D1709833

NO HANDS ALLOWED

A Robbie Reader

A Robbie Reader

Jay-Jay Okocha

Tamra Orr

Mitchell Lane
PUBLISHERS

P.O. Box 196
Hockessin, Delaware 19707
Visit us on the web: www.mitchelllane.com
Comments? email us: mitchelllane@mitchelllane.com

Mitchell Lane PUBLISHERS

Printing   1   2   3   4   5   6   7   8   9

A Robbie Reader
No Hands Allowed

Brandi Chastain	Brian McBride	DaMarcus Beasley
David Beckham	Freddy Adu	**Jay-Jay Okocha**
Josh Wolff	Landon Donovan	Michael Owen
Ronaldo	Robbie & Ryan Play Indoor Soccer	

Library of Congress Cataloging-in-Publication Data
Orr, Tamara.
    Jay-Jay Okocha / by Tamara Orr.
        p. cm. – (A Robbie reader. No hands allowed)
    Includes bibliographical references and index.
    ISBN 1-58415-493-4 (library bound: alk. paper)
    1. Okocha, Jay-Jay, 1973–Juvenile literature. 2. Soccer players–Nigeria–Biography–
Juvenile literature. I. Title. II. Series.
GV942.7.O46O77 2007
796.334092–dc22
[B]
                                                                      2006014811
ISBN-10: 1-58415-493-4   ISBN-13: 9781584154938

ABOUT THE AUTHOR: Tamara Orr is a full-time writer and author living in the Pacific Northwest. She has written more than 50 educational books for children and families, including *Orlando Bloom, Ice Cube,* and *Jamie Foxx* for Mitchell Lane Publishers. She is a regular writer for more than 50 national magazines and a dozen standardized testing companies. Orr is mother to four and life partner to Joseph.

PHOTO CREDITS: Cover–Alex Livesey/Getty Images; p. 4–Clive Brunskill/ALLSPORT; p. 6–Rick Stewart/ALLSPORT; p. 8 Alex Livesey/Getty Images; p. 10–Tony Ranze/AFP/Getty Images; p. 12–Issouf Sanogo/AFP/Getty Images; p. 15–Michael Steele/Getty Images; p. 16–Mark Thompson/Getty Images; p. 19–Laurence Griffiths/Getty Images; p. 20–Dave Benett/Getty Images; p. 22–John Stillwell/AFP/Getty Images; p. 24–Action Images/WireImage.com; p. 26–Karim Jaafar/AFP/Getty Images

ACKNOWLEDGMENTS: The following story has been thoroughly researched, and to the best of our knowledge represents a true story. While every possible effort has been made to ensure accuracy, the publisher will not assume liability for damages caused by inaccuracies in the data, and makes no warranty on the accuracy of the information contained herein. This story has not been authorized or endorsed by Jay-Jay Okocha or anyone associated with Jay-Jay Okocha.

TABLE OF CONTENTS

1/22/10 School Crossing(JS 20) 5.00

Jay-Jay's power running can be seen as he chases the ball down the field at the Nigerian soccer team's training camp in 1993.

An Unexpected Opportunity

It started out as just a simple visit. Augustine Okocha was 17 years old. He wanted to go to Germany and visit one of his brother's friends. It sounded like it would be fun. He knew the friend had played for a German football team. *Football* is the international word for soccer. Okocha loved the game. He had been playing it for as long as he could remember. Maybe he could learn a few new kicks or skills while he was there.

He had no idea that this quick visit would change his life, but it did. As soon as he got there, he asked his friend if he could go to soccer training with him. The answer was yes.

Jay-Jay battles with Italy's Roberto Donadoni during the 1994 World Cup match at Foxboro Stadium in Massachusetts.

Okocha watched all the players out on the field. He smiled. He knew he was as good as they were. He had been playing street soccer in Nigeria since he was little. Usually he did not have a real ball or an open field to play on either. Instead, he and other kids used the street and anything round enough to roll. It was not easy, but it was good training. He was sure he could do a great job on a real field with a real ball.

It did not take long for Okocha to ask if he could practice a little too. Once again, the answer was yes. By the second day, he had been invited to play with the team for two weeks.

At the end of that time, Okocha was registered with the Germans to be one of their main players. "It was all quite amazing," he says. "It never occurred to me that I was old enough to be on my own and start my own career. But I realized I had a big opportunity in front of me and knew that I didn't want to let it go. I knew I had to . . . grab the chance I'd been given."

Jay-Jay pauses a moment during a press conference before the 2004 Carling Cup finals. His team, the Bolton Wanderers, would play the final game against Boro (Middlesbrough) in the soaring Millenium Stadium in Cardiff, United Kingdom. In 1990, he had quickly advanced from playing street soccer to playing professionally.

Joining the Big Leagues

In just a matter of months, the young boy who only knew he loved to play street soccer was on his way to being a professional player. Most of his teammates were bigger and older than he was. That did not stop him.

"I think one of my strongest **assets** was that I was never afraid to play against people who were older than me," he remembers. "No matter what level I was playing at, I was never scared. When I got my opportunity, I never looked back. I wasn't afraid of anybody."

When he was growing up in Enugu, in southern Nigeria, Okocha had no idea that

his favorite game would one day be his career. He was born on August 14, 1973. His full name was Augustine Azuka Okocha, but sometimes he was called Austin. His family was fairly big. He had two brothers and four sisters.

All the men in the family liked to play soccer. Augustine loved the game! He was

Jay-Jay manages to tackle the ball from Hungary's Tamas Sandor during the first half of the game at the Florida Citrus Bowl in 1996.

always trying new tricks. He liked being able to do things that other players did not know how to do. When he was 13, he joined his school's team. There he learned how important it was to use his skills for helping his team instead of just showing off.

Less than a year after he signed up to play with Germany, Okocha was playing for Eintracht Frankfurt. This was one of the best clubs in the country. Over his years with Germany, he was able to score a goal 18 times. In 1993, one goal stood out among the rest. In the 87th minute of a game against Karlsruhe, he **dribbled** right through the entire defense and even past goalkeeper Oliver Kahn. This score was later voted as the Goal of the Year.

Showing off one of his best moves, Jay-Jay amazes two Senegalese players during the semifinal match of the 2002 Africa Cup of Nations soccer tournament.

CHAPTER THREE

A New Name

As each year went by, Okocha got busier. Soccer fans were watching him closely. They loved to see his dazzling dribbling skills.

After an argument with his coach, Okocha moved on to Turkey and joined a club called Fenerbahce. He continued to play the position of **midfielder**. During his years with his new team, he learned a lot about the game. He helped lead them to a surprise win against Manchester United. His team even achieved the Turkish League Championship that year.

Before Okocha began playing for Turkey, he also played for the Nigeria national football team. Their team was known as the Super Eagles. Okocha helped them win the 1994 Africa Cup of Nations. Two years later, he was also part of the team that won the gold medal at the Olympics in Atlanta! Even today, Okocha remembers that win as his favorite moment in his whole career. "Being the first African team to win the Olympic football tournament was a great feeling," he says. "It's difficult to describe how I felt. We never thought that we could win it but we did."

After a few years, however, Okocha was ready for something new. This time his eyes turned to Europe. France was looking right back! In 1998, Okocha signed up with a new club. This time it was for France's Paris St.-Germain. They offered an amazing $36 million for this fast dribbler. The deal made him the most well paid African player in the world.

Okocha was no longer known as Augustine or even Austin. Now he was called Jay-Jay. His

Surrounded by Birmingham's Nicky Butt (left) and Mehdi Nafti (right), Jay-Jay goes for the ball at Bolton's Reebok Stadium in 2006.

teammates said he was so good at the game, they had to name him twice.

He helped his new team reach the World Cup Finals. They won! It was the second time Okocha competed in this huge **tournament.** Fans from all over the world watched him fly across the field.

Jay-Jay kicks the ball over the head of Chelsea's Gianfranco Zola during the FA Barclaycard Premiership match in 2002.

Helping Others

In the summer of 2002, Okocha left the Paris team and joined the Bolton Wanderers in the United Kingdom. His first season started slowly. He got better with each game. It was not long before he was one of the team's top scorers. No one was surprised when he won the British Broadcasting Company (BBC) African Player of the Year award in 2003.

In November 2005, team owner Sam Allardyce said that Okocha was worth every single penny he had paid him. Indeed, Okocha was doing a great job. Following a game in which Okocha scored the winning goal,

Allardyce said, "It's a pleasure to have him and to watch his abilities on the field and to see how he helps bring the best out of the other people around him. The difference between us winning . . . was him alone. . . . From start to finish, he was the best man on the field."

Okocha was keeping very busy doing things other than playing soccer. He made a video called *Soccer Superskills with Jay-Jay Okocha.* It taught soccer skills to young people. The next year, he was made **ambassador** for SOS Children's Villages. This group helps take care of children who do not have families. Okocha and his wife, Nkechi, and their two

During a match in 2003, Jay-Jay reaches the ball just ahead of Sunderland's Sean Thornton.

Nkechi and Jay-Jay Okocha attend the FIFA 100 Best Players Party at London's Natural History Museum in 2004.

children visit there. They like to talk to the kids and give them some help.

Along with this honor, Okocha was named Nokia's People's Choice Player of the Tournament at the African Cup of Nations 2004. Africa soccer fans were asked to vote for their favorite player. More than 250,000 people voted. The biggest number of those votes was for Okocha. For each vote cast, one dollar was given to children in Nigeria.

The people from Nokia were very happy that Okocha won. They were sure that he deserved it. The director said, "Jay-Jay is a competitor and a true sportsman—traits that obviously connect with football fans from across the African continent."

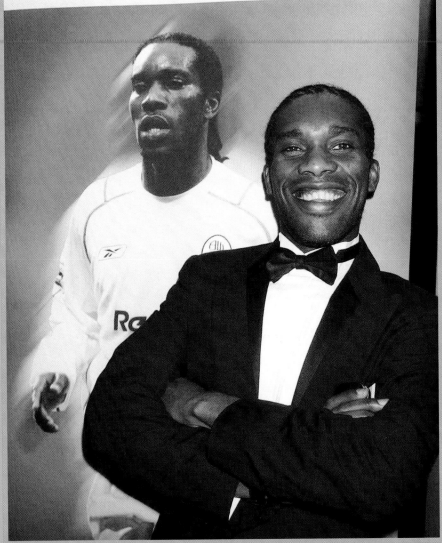

In 2004, Jay-Jay was honored to be nominated PFA Young Player of the Year. Although he didn't win this award, he won several others that year.

Looking to the Future

Okocha's career was going very well. In 2004, he won the BBC African Player of the Year again. He was the first player ever to win the award two years in a row. He was very happy about it. He was also pleased to find out that he had been named one of the world's best 100 **footballers.** He was one of the five Africans on the list.

In 2004, he signed up for three more years with Bolton. He was to be on their team at least through 2007. In early February 2006, however, he made an important announcement. He told his fans that he had decided to retire

At the Bolton School, Jay-Jay signs hundreds of T-shirts. He enjoys being a role model for kids.

from playing international soccer. He had helped the Nigerian Super Eagles reach third place in the Africa Cup of Nations. Now, he was ready to quit.

At least he thought he was. In July 2006, he changed his mind and joined the Qatar (kah-TAR) Sports Club for one year. "I decided to make Qatar Club my first choice because the conditions suit me. I'm having the best of times here. It's good to be here," said Okocha.

Okocha stays busy with his family. He hopes to eventually build a football school for Nigerian children. It is one way that he can share his passion for the sport with the love of his home country.

Okocha has important things to say to young kids today. "It is not necessarily if you play football, or are into other sports," he says. "In anything you have talent in and commit yourself, you are bound to succeed, with time. Success does not come in a jiffy and you don't

Jay-Jay battles Bahrain's Mohamed Ahmed Salmeen at a friendly match in Doha, Qatar, in 2006.

pluck it [from] a tree. Success comes from working hard and having some luck, as well."

It is little surprise that Okocha is loved by the children in Nigeria. They see him as a role model. To them, he says, "I want the kids to look at me and see in me what they can also become. I came out of a background of want, but today, I give the glory to God."

With his dazzling soccer skills, dedication to family, and passion for success, Okocha has a lot to be grateful for. Who knows what else the future might hold for him and the millions of fans who love to watch him?

1973 Okocha is born on August 14 in Enugu, Nigeria.

1986 He joins his school's soccer team.

1989 He joins his first club, Rangers International of Enugu.

1990 He goes to Germany and signs with Borussia Neunkirchen (Germany).

1992 He signs with Eintracht Frankfurt (Germany).

1994 He helps Nigeria win the Africa Cup of Nations; is on the winning World Cup team for the first time.

1996 He signs with Fenerbahce (Turkey). He also plays for Nigerian team that wins the gold medal at the Atlanta Olympics.

1998 His team wins the World Cup for the second time. He signs with Paris St.-Germain.

2002 His team wins the World Cup for the third time. He signs with the Bolton Wanderers in Bolton, United Kingdom.

2003 He is named BBC's African Player of the Year. He makes a soccer skills video.

2004 He renews his contract with Bolton Wanderers; is named Nokia's People's Choice Player of the Tournament; is made Ambassador of SOS Children's Villages; and is named BBC African Player of the Year for the second time.

2005   He is nominated for the BBC African Player of the Year award. Kevin Nolan replaces Jay-Jay as Bolton's captain.

2006   Okocha officially retires from international soccer competition and joins the Qatar Sports Club.

GLOSSARY

ambassador   (am-BAA-suh-dur)—an official representative or messenger.

asset   (AA-set)—a useful or valuable quality.

dribble   (DRIH-bul)—the primary way a player moves and controls the ball using his or her feet while running.

footballer   (FUT-bah-ler)—a person who plays soccer.

midfielder   (MID-feel-dur)—the player who helps the team by staying in the middle of the field to defend against a goal attempt.

tournament   (TUR-nuh-munt)—a series of contests in which teams compete against one another to see who is the ultimate winner.

FIND OUT MORE

Books

While there are no other books on Jay-Jay, you might enjoy reading the following soccer books from Mitchell Lane Publishers:

Brandi Chastain · *Brian McBride*
DaMarcus Beasley · *David Beckham*
Freddy Adu · *Josh Wolff*
Landon Donovan · *Michael Owen*
Ronaldo

Works Consulted

Akpododor, Gowon. "Okocha: Football Kept Me Away From My People." *The Guardian,* February 25, 2006. http://www.odili.net/news/source/2006/feb/25/16.html

BBC Manchester. "Africa Lives: Jay-Jay Okocha." April 7, 2005. http://www.bbc.co.uk/manchester/content/articles/2005/07/04 africa_okocha_040705_feature.shtml

BBC Sport Forum. "Jay-Jay Okocha Replies." December 13, 2001. http://news.bbc.co.uk/sport1/hi/sports_talk/forum/1706547.stm

Okocha, Jay-Jay, "My Lucky Break." http://news.bbc.co.uk/sportacademy/hi/sa/football/features/newsid_37210000/3721254/htm

The Independent: The Sport Channel. "Top Clubs and Agents in Dock Over TV Investigation," September 8, 2006. http://sport.independent.co.uk/football/bolton/article61254.ece

Memuletiwon, Ben. "Jay-Jay Okocha: New King in the Land of Soccer Blinds." *[Nigeria] Daily Sun,* July 24, 2006. http://www.sunnewsonline.com/webpages/sports/2006/july/24/sports-24-07-2006-003.htm

Nokia Press Release. "Jay-Jay Okocha Named Nokia's 'People's Choice Player of the Tournament.'" February 14, 2004. http://press.nokia.com/PR/200402/934407_5.html

Olajire, Ademola. "My Legacy." All Africa.com http://allafrica.com/stories/printable/200602200037.html

Soccernet. http://soccernet.espn.go.com/print?id=1-863&type=player&cc=5901

Sharrock, Gordon. "Bye, Bye to Jay-Jay." *Bolton Evening News,* May 9, 2006 http://www.boltoneveningnews.co.uk/search/display.var.754618.0.bye_bye_to_jay_jay.php

SOS Children's Villages http://www.sos-hildrensvillages.org/

The Sport Network. "Jay-Jay Okocha." http://www.sportnetwork.net/main/s474/st77863.htm

Web Addresses
Super Eagles Home
http://www.supereagles.com/
Bolton Wanderers home page
http://www.bwfc.premiumtv.co.uk/
A profile of Okocha
http://www.jayjayokocha.info/